All Familiar Things Were Once Strange

Sophia Joan Short

THOUGHT
CATALOG
Books

THOUGHTCATALOG.COM
NEW YORK · LOS ANGELES

THOUGHT CATALOG Books

This book was produced by Chris Lavergne and Noelle Beams with art direction and design by KJ Parish. Special thanks to Bianca Sparacino for creative editorial direction and Isidoros Karamitopoulos for circulation management.

Visit us at thoughtcatalog.com and shopcatalog.com.

Made in the United States of America.

ISBN 978-1-949759-41-9

Published by Thought Catalog Books, an imprint of the digital magazine Thought Catalog, which is owned and operated by The Thought & Expression Company LLC, an independent media organization based in Brooklyn, New York and Los Angeles, California.

For my Granny
who was the best at giving pep talks
(and those who miss hearing them).

Hi there—Glad you opened up this book. Now, these poems aren't meant to be a guide or give instructions for your life, but hope, encouragement, and feeling less alone are what they might provide. And maybe they can be alongside as you tackle what's next for you in this big game that we call life. Even though we don't have the same day-to-day, I hope you find some familiar feelings reflected to you on these pages. I've written words about the major themes in my life so far—finding the courage to try something new, the relationship with yourself and others, mental health, growing up, and the future. These words might hold some truth for you and even make that little spark of hope grow a bit brighter as you write the pages for your story.

There's no right way to read this book—maybe you flip to a random page or tear out a poem that speaks to your current life stage. Reread it a hundred times or get halfway through and decide to give it to a friend who it might serve more than you. Maybe you finish it once and then leave a page on a different car windshield every weekend for the next few months, fold up your favorite poem and slide it under your neighbor's door, or leave it in the bathroom of a random gas station on your next vacation.

In all seriousness, however you read it, I'm deeply grateful that you're taking the time to. Hope these words hold some meaning for you.

Lots of love,
Sophia

Courage is
doing your
best when
there is no
guarantee
for success.

On Trying Things

If we're going to get to know each other—I'll be honest up front. I like to be the best right away at stuff—and when I'm not, the feelings that settle in are tough. But something that I've been reminded an embarrassing number of times is that success isn't usually the first thing that I find. Instead it's a process of trying, failing, and trying again, and that's exactly what you'll find words in this chapter saying. So many perceptions that we hold make you feel like you're failing harder than you actually are—not having the whole picture, comparing your beginning to someone else's middle, or thinking you should have succeeded on the first try. The good news is you can look at every failure as something that provides a little padding so the next one doesn't bruise your ego quite as badly. Don't get me wrong—it probably will still sting a little, but for me, the more failures I've collected, the easier time I have getting back up and understanding it's just a step to getting where I'm going.

For when you're starting something new

If something could go wrong, it could also go right—

So start shaky

Start unsure

You're writing a brave beginning to this chapter

A case for beginning

Being a beginner doesn't mean you're bad at something
it means that there's space to grow
Sometimes that space seems so big
Filled with so much to learn and know
And of course you'll make mistakes
But the biggest one would be not to try
Because the time you spend wondering about it
Will still pass by

Time

Remember all the familiar things
that were once strange—
Like
The commute to work you can do with your eyes closed
when at first you relied on Google Maps for every turn
The skill you never thought you would learn
Or the layout of a new home you can
now navigate in the dark

It's possible for any big unsettling change
To transform
Because time has a funny way of
making an uphill climb unfold
Into a simple stroll through the park

When we
cling to
what we know,
we miss
how we
could
grow

For when you hear no

The beauty of a no is hardly ever immediate—
If you thought the job was yours—
there's a another one waiting
The person you thought was forever—
well, there's someone better
The idea you thought would immediately
click just needs more time to make it tick
Being told no often feels like the ending
When in fact
Something greater is just beginning

For the perfectionist

Making mistakes mean that you're
perfect at being human

For when you mess up

Your next step after a mistake matters
more than that you made one

Hands-On Learner

Eating salsa in a white bathrobe
Cutting your own bangs or
Rubbing instead of blotting that stain
Washing a nonstick pan when it's hot
Or taking a job you pretend is right even
though your gut says it's not
Getting a ticket for driving too fast
Or promising yourself that
The chance you're giving them is the last
It's unfortunate but true
That sometimes you have to make the mistake
For the lesson to be memorable for you

Maybe
this time
was
about
learning—
next time
can be
about
the result

For when you feel overwhelmed

You don't have to be good at everything right now

(or ever)

On the first draft

The first try might be terrible
But getting started is what
Makes getting better possible

Success

Success is sometimes good luck—
But it's usually hard work added up
And some failures
An occasional oh what the f*ck
Plus a lot of self-doubt
But those pieces are never what we talk about

So the next time you see someone win
(even when jealousy is what you feel)
Start clapping
Because you don't know all the tough places they've been
After all, you're just looking through their highlight reel

Making
mistakes
means
you're perfect
at being
human

For when things don't go as planned

Maybe this time was about learning

Next time can be about the result

Happy Spring

Blooming is a process
Sometimes
Before you realize
That bit by bit
You're in the middle of it

Give yourself
a little credit

Once we've arrived,

we tend to forget how much work it took to get there

For when success doesn't feel like you thought it would

It's weird to realize the journey is sometimes
more interesting than the destination.
What you saw and who you met along the way
Might be more important than the final view
If that's what you find—maybe it's
because your mind knows
This wasn't your peak
Get moving
You've got further to go

Something to remember

See the value in your success
but know your worth isn't based on it
You're so much more than your wins and losses

If
you
weren't
ready,

you
wouldn't
have
the
opportunity

On Yourself

The relationship you have with yourself affects all the others. Read that again. We'll get to other people as well as mental health in the coming chapters, but in this one, I just want you to take stock of a couple of things: how you're speaking to yourself and if you really feel comfortable in your own skin. No matter what's going on outside of you, if you're hypercritical of yourself, life is going to feel uncomfortable—everything will be put through a lens that's too sharp. Secondly, if you don't feel like yourself—maybe you're trying to be someone that you feel like the world will like better—that gnawing feeling of faking it will always be present. Most of all, I want you to know that you're worthy of love—especially from yourself. So maybe scribble these words and slap them on a post-it note on your mirror so whenever you glance up you'll see someone worthy of that.

Focus on
this first

The relationship you have with
yourself affects all the others
Your eyes, after all, are the ones
you see the world through.
If you see good in yourself
You might find it in others too

About
your body

What if you said "thank you" to your body instead?

Your lungs

Your legs

Your heart

Your brain

Your skin

Your stomach

And all of their fellow parts

are quietly putting in 168 hour work weeks—unpaid

So at least do me a favor

And don't let your thoughts beat up your body today

This one goes out to my acne, cellulite, and stretch marks

It only becomes a flaw
when you treat it like one.

Where can you soften?

Can you treat yourself with softness
when things are hard?
Because life will never be easy
But loving yourself harder
might make it easier

The relationship you have with yourself affects all the others

Belonging

Stop trying to fit in places that
make you leave a piece of yourself out

Belonging Part II

If you feel like you're too much or too little
maybe you're adding yourself to the wrong recipe

Weird

Maybe what makes you weird is
why you're in the world—
You might as well let it out because
there's only one chance
for it to know someone just like you

Top 40

Sometimes we're so plugged in
We're out of tune with ourselves
So stop your scrolling, hit pause
See what thoughts
Are at the top
Of your brainwaves' charts

Life
is too short
to be mean
to yourself.

Be the first

Be brave enough to bet on yourself
It'll attract people that believe in you too

Who's Running This Meeting, Anyway?

Listen to how you speak to yourself
It is the one voice you'll always hear
Notice which tone is hogging all the time
in the meeting inside your head
If Cruel is front and center
Remind them Kindness is on the agenda today instead

In summary

If I could sum up what this whole
chapter is trying to say:
Life is too short to be mean to yourself.

Can you
treat
yourself
with
softness
when
things
are hard?

On Other People

I'm an introvert. I know, an introvert who enjoys writing—not shocking news. Extroverts, skip over this next sentence—I need to spend time alone and often crave it, but you've got to have other people. I know my life is better because of a lot of people—some that I text everyday, some that slid in and out of my life, and some I've never met. But not every person is lovely and that's okay. Some people will be unpleasant, or downright mean, but they're still a part of your life, and sometimes I find myself learning as much from them as people that I enjoy.

The final thing that I'll say before getting into the poems is that sometimes we have no idea how much of an impact we have on other people—and I can only imagine the same is true with other people and their relationship to you. So maybe take some time and send them a "thank you for being you" out of the blue.

One of life's greatest miracles

Think about all the things that had to go right so
you could meet some of your favorite people—
Whoever popped into your head
And brought out that little smile
Deserves a call right now
(or text if that's more your style)
Even if it's been a while

Powerful

The people that are quickest to flash
The exotic places that they've been
Positions of power that they've held
And put all the shiny pieces of their life on display
Are the ones that should be asked
But are you happy—actually happy
With yourself right now?

Old Friends

You grew up down the street
and your lives look different now
But
They knew you when you talked
about Harry Potter on repeat
Tried to see how much birthday cake you could eat
And cared too much about who your
soccer team would beat

They knew you before you worried about making rent
And paying taxes
And if you're making the right career advances

And maybe they're the ones who got you know you best
Before you began silencing pieces of yourself
Instead of speaking them out loud

New Friends

Of course they won't know
That you sleep with white noise cranked really loud
And that your little brother makes you proud

And how could they know
That you spent years only using forks of plastic
And until fifth grade all of your pants were elastic

On meeting you they won't know your family's history
Or the chapters that make you sad from your story

And not all of the new people that
pass through your life will stick
But it's worth giving the chance to let some
New friends become old ones

Very rarely am I the only character in my best memories.

Hold the door

People can make your day better or worse
Which means you can do the same

2020

A bad situation is the best time
To be good to one another
While we can't control what happens
We can keep choosing to be kind

Running

One Saturday I passed a stranger who was running down
the trail I was running up
(noticeably out of breath)
They yelled to me—
"You're almost at the top—don't stop!"
And I think about that two second exchange
Every time I have the chance to give
Encouragement an invitation
To be part of a conversation

Assumptions

I spent a year being critical of a
classmate in the 12th grade
Mostly based on assumptions I had made
As we sat down about to graduate
Chatting to pass the time
Before we turned our tassels
I realized what I thought I knew about
their home, family and life was just not the case
It's strange that we keep taking the sliver
of a person's life that we know
And keep filling in our information
To make the story our brain made up whole

People
can make
your day better
or worse

Which
means you
can do
the same

Racism

Silence gives room hate to grow
Speaking up can start to shrink it

Home

It's okay to outgrow
Who or what once felt like home
But one of the hardest things to know
Is when it's time to let those keys go

On giving people a second chance

Every time I swear I won't hit it off with someone
I think of the girl in my kindergarten class
Who stole the rubber giraffe from me at playtime
And even made me cry
It's funny because
After all this time
I had the honor of standing up for her
as she walked down the aisle last July .

When you don't understand someone

You probably don't share everything about you—
so let's not assume everything about them
What might look like the worst
Might be the best they can give right now

Maybe
the
whole
point
is to
figure out
how to
help
someone
else.

On tough people

Perhaps some people are placed in your life
So you can figure out exactly what you don't want to be
And some so you can see who you want to become
We don't get to choose who marks on us
in pencil or permanent marker
But we can keep choosing if we color our actions
with Kindness or something harsher

Most of mine make me laugh

Very rarely am I the only character in my best memories
And that means the special moment survives somewhere
Besides my brain alone
And makes that person feel a little more like home

On
feeling seen

The ones you can laugh and cry with
are the ones you should closely hold
Because when you share either a tear or a joke
It's like sharing a little piece of your soul

No one's paying as much attention as you think

We get scared of what people will think—
But they do not think twice about it
We waste so much time bracing
for an imaginary reaction
That we'll never get

The point

Maybe the point of this is to figure
out how to help someone else
But when you don't know where to start
Remember a lot of small moments changed you

so

Maybe you don't need to give a speech
just encourage someone in conversation
Maybe you don't need to donate a fortune
just pay for someone's lunch one day
Maybe you don't need to write a best-selling novel
just write a friend a letter
And maybe you will create an impact
through a thousand small acts

Think about
all the things
that had
to go right
so you
could
meet
some of
your favorite
people—

On your thoughts

Much like you, I spend a lot of time thinking even when I don't mean to. Sometimes my thoughts appear and they're the ones that I would like to stick around—they're the ones I have the easiest time talking about, when I'm feeling grateful, content, joyful—basically all things that might be labeled as "positive." Something that people often get wrong about me is that I never have a negative thought or a bad day, but that's very far from true. I just have a harder time expressing emotions like grief, loneliness, heartbreak and often (okay, always) would rather make a joke or smile instead of speaking these feelings aloud. But something I'm learning—and often process through writing—is that having space to allow yourself to feel both is important. So buckle up, baby— over the next few pages come some words about good feelings and some bad ones—there's one in here that was the only thing I cried at while writing. Whatever state you find yourself reading these in—know you're not alone in experiencing what you're feeling.

For tough times

When everything is uncertain
everything that's important becomes clear

On gratitude

When you find one thing to be grateful for
it's easier to find another

It's impossible
to know
how life
will ebb
and flow

But
you're worth
the highs &
strong enough
to push through
the lows

Let it out

When we hold emotions in
Our thoughts start to stir them
Until they're like a can of Coke shaken up—
And when life drops in a new point
of pressure like a Mento
There's no telling how you'll explode

Monday was bad, Friday was good

I had a week not too long ago
Where Monday started with being
yelled at over the phone
And Friday ended with a raise
(Tuesday, Wednesday, Thursday were all just okay)
It's impossible to know how life will ebb and flow
But you're worth the highs and strong
enough to push through the lows

My favorite question to ask

Is what you're holding onto worth
the space it's taking up?
Now when I say space
I don't mean that growing pile of clutter in the corner
Or that stack of papers you're holding onto just in case
What I really mean is the conversation from
earlier that you keep replaying in your head
Or picturing tomorrow's to-do list with dread
I'm talking about the thoughts that leave you staring
at the ceiling wondering if you're good enough
Or if life will always feel this tough
Most of the time
you're letting the future and past take up so much room
There's little space to see what's right in front of you

Check what's going on inside too

It's so easy to get distracted
With an endless stream of scrolling, shows, and songs
that keep your mind occupied all day long
Ticking accomplishments off your list
Or raging at the driver that cut you off in traffic
Finishing the laundry pile
Or starting awake in the middle of night wondering
oh god did I have something in my
teeth at lunch when I smiled?
Life is loud and moves so fast
That it's up to us to spot our thoughts
and feelings that slide quietly past

Look around you

When you want a special life
Remember
Maybe the amount of extraordinary
things that happen in your life
Depends on what you notice

Why I go to therapy

The thing about keeping heavy secrets
You think no one will understand
Is the pressure will start to seep into your life
And weaken the foundation
So before you start to crumble
Try to tell one person
And you might be surprised that
brick by brick
The crushing weight might start to lift

Anxiety

Dreading the short days of winter
Before the start of spring
Tossing and turning all night afraid
You won't hear your alarm play
Finding success and instead of enjoying it
wondering when will I be able to do this again?
This is how I would summarize anxiety—
Your brain hating the future before it even begins

Maybe the
amount of
extraordinary
things that
happen in
your life

Depends
on what
you notice

Story of My Life

You smile a lot

        I smile when I'm nervous

And then I grinned again.

A Natural Disaster

More often than not
The pain of losing someone doesn't
end with the first big shock
Grief is found in the tremors
When you have good news to share
But they aren't there
Or maybe you move to a new place
And can't invite them to come stay
Sometimes it's felt
When you take side streets instead of the highway
Just because doing something they would
Makes you feel a little closer to them that day
A small wave might pass through
When you see someone with the same
knee scar or driving their exact car
None of this will make their death less painful
But maybe this is how to understand the magnitude
Of how much they meant to you

Trauma

Sometimes I think we're sad for no reason
Because we didn't let ourselves feel when there was one

Thoughts

The mind is an open door
Impossible to control what thoughts enter
But when depression, self-harm or whatever
monsters that have a habit of creeping in
Can you say hello but not feed them
with all your attention

Doubled Over

You've got to find out what makes you laugh
(like the can't-stop-laughing-because-trying-
to-stop-only-makes-it-funnier kind)
Because life builds in ways to make you cry

Superglue

If things feel broken
maybe it's so you can glue something
better back together
with the pieces

Go Outside

Get outside—
Of your head
Of your home
Of the limits you've carefully
constructed around your life

Small Talk

Before we were about to land
The lady sitting next to me on the
plane asked what I was writing
(I think her phone was dying)
"Oh, I write some poems for fun"
"Ah, I thought you were making a to-
do list, a really long one"
And in the car home—
I realized she was at least half right
The poems are my thoughts and feelings—
Some puffy, white—gently floating by
Some stormy and turbulent, swirling to
create a hurricane in my mind—
And both I don't want—
But *need*
To get out of my brain
So my pen rescues them midair
and ensures a safe landing on the page

Is what you're
holding onto
worth the
space
it's taking
up?

On growing up

So I'm getting to that stage in life where it feels like big, heavy choices are being made. I'm watching people I love get married, have babies, start businesses—all tentpole moments that aren't as easy to change as your major in college or bad choice of seventh-grade side bangs. Even if we're not the same age, what I want to explore over the next few pages is what growing up feels like. See, I used to think that growing up was something I would quite literally outgrow—but instead, I think it's more about what goes on inside your head. When you notice that you're no longer who you used to be, that nothing was the same as a few years ago, that everything around you has changed. But maybe it's a time to realize too that this means there's room for a different, more complete version of you. No matter if you've made it to 17, 73, or 25 like me, I think there's more room to grow into a fuller version of yourself for however many more years you'll get on this planet.

On the next few pages you'll find my thoughts—some steeped in nostalgia—on what growing up feels like so far and maybe, more importantly, thinking about who I want to be.

Growing up

I used to think there was an age where
I would have it all figured out
When I'd be a real adult
I'd have a job and house and a forever partner
I'd wear tailored clothes and drive a shiny car

But I still have acne at twenty-five
And keep buying plants I don't know how to keep alive
Last week I had an infestation of fruit flies
—which are mostly gone by the way—
And I wear leggings to my corporate job everyday

But I'm learning to trust where my real worth lies
And I do know when my taxes are due
It's okay if I don't fall in love with a dude
I know that I like to cook
And that I want to write this book
So maybe the point isn't to reach a
destination of being a grown up
But to keep growing into yourself

Would
six-year-old you be proud?
Adjust accordingly.

I bet they didn't grow up dreaming for

the answer to "how are you"

To always be "busy"

Or taking a job that you really hate

Just to see how much money you can make

What might make them sad

Is the time you spent feeling guilty over that slice of cake

And that you can't make time to play

Or even notice what excites you today

Sure you might know more than them now

But sometimes it takes talking to someone

Who knew you all of those years ago

To see what shape your life is taking

And if it's time to change the choices you're making

Home for the holidays

When you find yourself somewhere
That you used to know
Old memories roll past
And it might be tempting to linger on one
wishing that time would have lasted
So when you see the familiar streets
that used to be home
Also take a moment to pause and admire how much
You've grown

A list of things
that make me sad

Growing older and moving away from friends
And realizing that you'll never go to a sleepover
at each other's childhood homes again

That there's so much divide in the world and in
between either side the hatred only seems to grow

That we're using up oil, water, and plastic, like
the Earth is able to support our habits

That people I love are gone and that you only feel the
hole when you realize your heart has one without them

That I know more than I used to

A list of things
that make me glad

Getting to know friends through every stage
and watching them blossom with age

That we may not be able to completely
bridge the divide, but sometimes it's possible
to stick a hand out to the other side

That there might be time to start using
less oil, water, and plastic, and the Earth
might heal from our bad habits

That I'm still waiting to meet people who
will unlock different parts of my heart

That I know more than I used to

Maybe
it's time
you created
your
normal

Choices

We're fonder of choices
We've seen made before
But it's okay to listen to the voice
Asking for something different
Something more

I didn't recycle
until I moved to New York

Start separating familiar from good—
Familiarity can give us a false sense of safety
When in reality it's building a box around
your life with walls made from materials
that aren't good for you at all

Trust yourself

You can listen to someone's opinion about your life
Just remember you're the one living it
We get so caught up with
What other people will think
Instead of remembering
there's a capable brain inside our heads

While you're writing it,

Can you find one thing from this chapter that you'll miss?

Oh that piece of yourself? You'll find it again

Maybe the best part of getting older
Is picking back up the pieces of ourselves
we've lost along the way
So you'll find that creativity or
confidence or sense of humor or
whatever piece of you
That's been hidden away

Growing pains

It's okay to outgrow what used to feel like home
But sometimes we hold onto the keys just in case
Instead of letting them go

Take a trip back to you

Maybe growing up
Is shedding all of the somebodies
we tried to become
So we can remember
who we really are

Cool

Being cool is a shine that wears off over time
And when that starts to fade away
What's inside is put on display

One of the biggest ways to waste your life

Is wishing you had somebody else's

Normal

What's considered normal is just something
that's been made up by people
And you're a person
So maybe it's time you created your normal

Fart Jokes Forever

There's nothing more boring than people
who take themselves too seriously
So no matter how important you get
How to laugh at yourself is something not to forget

You've got to use the one you've got

One of the biggest ways to waste your life
Is wishing you had somebody else's

It's okay
to outgrow
what
used to
feel like
home

Before it's gone

There won't be a first time
you feel the independence (and panic)
of signing your first lease again
Or the excitement when you get off the airplane
in a new city ready for your adult life to begin

You won't enter the workforce
And spend your lunch breaks in the
aisles of Trader Joe's on 23rd
Offering (questionable) and receiving (good) advice
from your fellow recent grads twice

There won't be another first FaceTime call from a
friend telling you they're going to walk down the aisle
Or the conversation when your cousin tells
you they're about start trying for a child

And quietly there might be the spark of realization
that where you grew up is no longer home

And maybe your life is about be better
than you could have known

There's usually no fanfare or graduation ceremony
When you move on from a small moment
that holds great significance

So while you're writing it,
Can you find one thing from this
chapter that you'll miss?

On what's next

Who honestly knows? The future holds so much space for uncertainty and—well—that's enough to keep me up at night. Maybe it's because I like to plot things out, carefully craft my next step, and—I'll just say it—be in control. But as I've been reminded again and again, the best and the worst things are going to come up unexpectedly. Bad stuff is coming that will blindside you, but there are also good people waiting to meet you and good things that you will create. Over the next few pages, you'll find some words about hope. Maybe if one speaks to you, rip it out and stick it in your pocket when you're about to tackle something scary—just a little confidence boost from me to you.

When you need to know
something good is up ahead

Trust your hard work is unlocking

doors you can't see yet

Imposter Syndrome

If you weren't ready
You wouldn't have the opportunity

What's Next

We get worried about what comes next
but forget that now used to be next
So chances are you're more than capable
Of handling what's around the corner

Life
is just a
string
of moments

And
right now
is one
of them

For when life feels sticky

You're not stuck—

You're learning

You're growing

You're preparing to bloom

Zoom out
(out out out)

If you feel like you aren't growing think
about where you were a year ago—
Maybe you're examining your life on
a lens that's so zoomed in
You've already outgrown it

Look ahead

Is this as good as it gets?

Maybe.

But you've got to keep going if you want to know

One Step

When you feel overwhelmed
And that you set the bar for your dreams too high
Remember you just need enough bravery
For the next step
Not the whole staircase
So keep those dreams as high in the sky
But your feet on the ground
Step by step climbing no matter your pace

Be proud
of how far
you've
come

Even if
it's not
where you
thought you
would be

Comparison

Comparison places a limit on what your life can become
When we only strive for what we know
We forget we're capable of more than we can imagine

Keep what's
important to you close

When you hold anything too tightly
We squeeze the joy right out of it
I'll be the first to admit
when my life lacks laughter, love, or a reason to smile
Even the greatest success doesn't feel worthwhile

Go make that thing

Celebrating creativity is practice
honoring a different point of view
So the next time you're scared of sharing
that little spark inside of you
Uncover it and let it glow
Because it might change how someone
sees the world more than you know

You're
not
stuck–

You're
learning

You're
growing

You're
preparing
to bloom

It's been a longggg road

Be proud of how far you've come
Even if it's not where you thought you would be—
There were mountains you didn't see coming
Yet you made it over them
Waves so big you weren't sure if you would ever breathe
And sharp curves in the road that slowed you down
but you still made it around
So give yourself a little credit because
you survived much more than what was planned

Once I left my wallet on my car seat

Sometimes Change rams violently
—unexpectedly—
Shattering a version of your life
Like a heavy hammer being taken to your car
window you once saw the world through
You've got to decide what to do as the glass spider
web of shards become increasingly unsteady
You can grab hold of the scattered pieces
convinced you can patch together what you once knew
Or worse, armor yourself with the spiky slivers
Ready to fight anything unfamiliar, anything new
Or maybe you carefully toss the pieces in the trash—
(Knowing you'll find glimmering chips of
your past in your cupholders and underneath
floor mats even if you use a shock vac)
And steady yourself to embrace
What's different
Because, well, it might be new,
But this is a valuable piece of your life too

Tick Tock

If you ever think little things don't add up
Remember seconds make up your life
because
Life is just a string of moments
And right now is one of them
We all get a first sunrise
But don't know when the last will come
So stop waiting—your life has already begun

You
just need
enough bravery

For the
next step

Not the whole
staircase

Ending

Well, you've made it to the end. Usually I'm not a fan of goodbyes—book endings, airport gates, and the song that they play at graduation ceremonies all want to make me cry. But my favorite part of poetry is that this isn't the end of the ride. Each time you return to a poem, it can hold a new meaning in the context of your life's story. It can also be a good time to revisit the version of you who read those words during a different chapter and reflect on what happened after.

So my gratitude for everyone that's made this book possible doesn't end with this page either. Friends, family, and strangers on the internet who have encouraged me to write—whether that's been through an Instagram like or giving me advice in real life. And of course, thank you to Team Thought Catalog for taking a chance and sorting through many ideas and drafts.

Sophia Joan Short is a writer, author, yoga teacher, and social media strategist living in Los Angeles. Inspired by the connective power of emotion, Sophia is committed to using words to encourage others to write their own life story. When she's not writing, you can find her exploring nature or experimenting in the kitchen.

instagram.com/sophia.joan.short

sophiajshort.com

MORE FROM
THOUGHT CATALOG BOOKS

The Stength In Our Scars
—Bianca Sparacino

The Mountain Is You
—Brianna Wiest

Everything You'll Ever Need
(You Can Find Within Yourself)
—Charlotte Freeman

Your Heart Is The Sea
—Nikita Gill

**THOUGHT
CATALOG**
Books

THOUGHTCATALOG.COM
NEW YORK · LOS ANGELES